유나와 호기심 많은 모든 아이들에게 –
꿈꾸는 것을 멈추지 마.

For Yoona, and all the other young curious minds.
Never stop dreaming.

미야자키 하야오

Hayao Miyazaki

옛날에 일본 도쿄에 미야자키 하야오라는 소년이 있었어요.
하야오의 아빠는 비행기 부품을 만드는 공장에서 일하셔서,
하야오는 어려서부터 비행기를 보고 그리는 것을 좋아했어요.

Once upon a time, in Tokyo, Japan, there was a little boy named Hayao Miyazaki. His dad worked at a company that made airplane parts, so Hayao grew up watching airplanes and loved drawing them, too.

하야오의 엄마는 자주 아프셨기 때문에 병원에서 많은 시간을 보냈어요. 하지만 늘 밝고, 활발하고, 용감하게 병과 싸우셨죠.

Hayao's mom was often very sick and spent a lot of time in the hospital. Despite this, she was bright, lively, and bravely fighting her illness.

이런 엄마를 보면서 하야오는 어려움을 딛고 세상을 구하는, 다정하고 강인한 여전사를 상상했어요.

These experiences filled Hayao with dreams of kind yet strong heroines who could overcome all obstacles and save the world.

하야오는 커가면서 애니메이션을 좋아하게 되었어요. 어느 날
한 애니메이션에 나온 용감한 소녀를 보고 흠뻑 빠진 하야오는,
나중에 커서 저런 이야기를 만들어야겠다고 결심했어요.

As he got older, Hayao loved movies, especially animations.
One day, a brave little girl in an animated film captivated
him, and he decided to make his own stories.

그래서 하야오는 대학을 졸업한 후 애니메이션
스튜디오에서 일하기 시작했어요. 하야오가 그린
재미있는 이야기들은 일본의 어린이들이 무척
좋아했어요.

After college, Hayao worked at an animation
studio. He thought up and drew lots of
exciting stories, and kids in Japan loved them.

물론 하야오의 모든 애니메이션이 인기가 있었던 건 아니에요. 열심히 준비해서 만든 한 애니메이션이 실패했을 때 하야오는 크게 실망했어요.

However, not all of his animations were successful. When one movie he had worked really hard on became a flop, Hayao felt sad and disappointed.

하지만 하야오는 포기해서는 안된다고 생각했어요. 그래서 뭔가 다른 것을 해보기로 결심했죠. 바로 자신만의 독특한 스타일로 그린 만화 시리즈였어요.

But he knew he couldn't give up. He decided to try something different—a cartoon series in his own unique style.

이 시리즈는 나중에 멋진 영화로 만들어졌어요. 세상을 구하는 용감한 소녀, '나우시카'의 이야기였죠. 나우시카는 하야오가 오랫동안 상상해왔던 여전사였어요. 많은 사람들은 이 영화를 좋아하고 칭찬했어요.

This series grew into a beautiful movie about a brave girl named *Nausicaä* who tries to save her world, just as he had imagined for a long time. Many people loved and praised it.

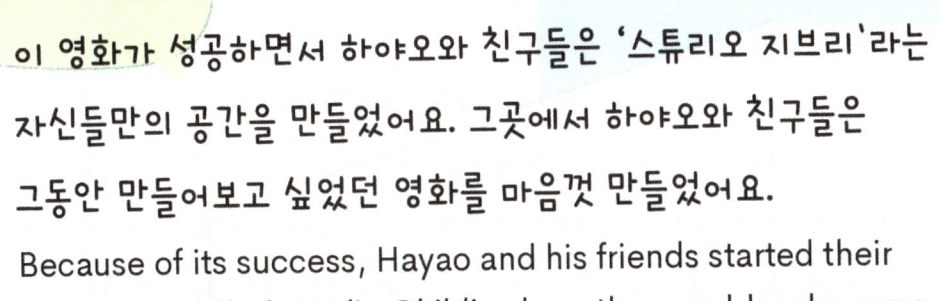

이 영화가 성공하면서 하야오와 친구들은 '스튜리오 지브리'라는 자신들만의 공간을 만들었어요. 그곳에서 하야오와 친구들은 그동안 만들어보고 싶었던 영화를 마음껏 만들었어요.

Because of its success, Hayao and his friends started their own place called *Studio Ghibli*, where they could make more movies the way they wanted.

스튜디오 지브리에서 하야오는 유명한 영화, '이웃집 토토로'를 만들었어요. 두 자매와 거대하고, 신비로운 생명체인 토토로의 이야기였죠.

At *Studio Ghibli*, Hayao created the famous movie, *My Neighbor Totoro*, about two sisters and a giant, friendly magical creature called Totoro.

이 영화에서는 멋진 자연과 우정을 아름답게 보여줬어요. 놀랍게도 토토로는 어른과 아이들 모두에게 사랑받는 문화 아이콘이 되었어요.

This movie beautifully depicted friendship and the wonders of nature. To everyone's surprise, Totoro became a cultural icon, beloved by children and adults alike.

하지만 하야오는 많은 어려움에 부딪혔어요. 때로는 하야오의 생각이 사람들이 기대했던 것과 너무 달랐거든요.

However, Hayao faced many challenges. Sometimes, his ideas were quite different from what other people expected.

그래서 어떤 사람들은 하야오의 영화를 좋아했지만, 어떤 사람들은 아이들이 보기에 너무 추상적이고 어렵다고 생각했어요. 하지만 하야오는 계속 나아갔어요.

Some people liked his work, but others thought it was too complicated or abstract for children. Regardless, Hayao kept pushing forward.

하야오는 주변에 재능 있는 아티스트와 작가들을 모았어요.
이들은 열심히 일하고, 서로 격려해 주면서 많은 사람들에게 감동을
주는 멋진 이야기를 만드는 데 집중했죠.

He surrounded himself with other talented artists and
storytellers. They worked hard, supported each other,
and focused on creating even more amazing stories
that touched the hearts of many.

하야오와 친구들이 만든 모든 영화에는 모험과 멋진 그림이 가득했어요.

Each film Hayao and his friends made was filled with adventure and beautiful pictures.

하야오의 영화는 유명한 국제 시상식에서 상을 받고, 세계 많은 사람들에게 일본 애니메이션의 아름다움을 알렸어요.

His movies started winning renowned international awards and introduced global fans to the unique beauty of Japanese storytelling.

하야오는 세계적으로 유명해졌어요. 하야오가 가는 곳마다 사람들은 하야오를 환영했고, 하야오가 만든 영화를 보고 싶어 했어요. 하지만 하야오는 그림 그리는 것을 좋아했던 어린 시절의 꿈을 잊지 않았어요.

Hayao became famous all over the world. People eagerly welcomed him everywhere he went, excited to see his next creation. But he always remembered his dreams as a little boy who loved to draw.

하야오는 상상하는 것들이 멋진 모험이 될 수 있다는 것을 가르쳐주었어요. 우리가 해야 하는 것은, 우리의 꿈을 믿고, 열심히 노력하고, 포기하지 않는 거예요. 하야오 영화의 여전사처럼요.

Hayao taught us that our imaginations can lead to great adventures. All we need to do is believe in our dreams, work hard, and never give up—just like the heroes in his movies.

Hayao Miyazaki's
Masterpieces

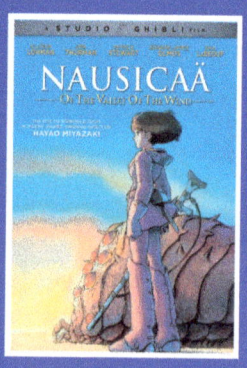

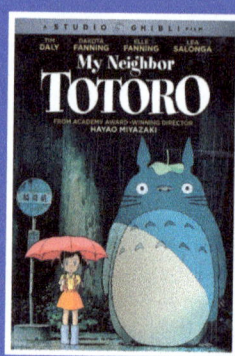

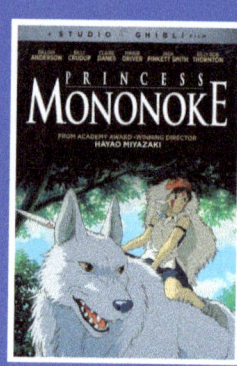

1984

Nausicaä of the Valley of the Wind

1988

My Neighbor Totoro

1997

Princess Mononoke

In many of Hayao Miyazaki's stories, the main characters are often girls. They are lovely but also bold and brave, ready to solve big problems. Hayao dreamed of a world where strong girls lead the way. Many people loved his idea of girl power, especially since it was unusual at the time.

My Neighbor Totoro was very popular in Japan and loved by animation fans around the world. But it was *Princess Mononoke* that made him famous everywhere.

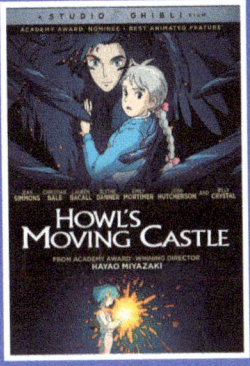

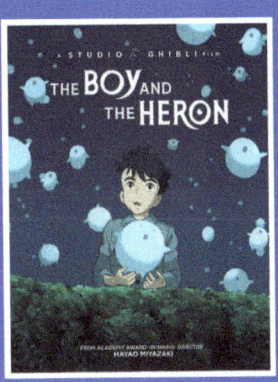

2001	2004	2023
Spirited Away	Howl's Moving Castle	The Boy and The Heron

After that, *Spirited Away* came out, and people all over the world praised it as a wonderful masterpiece. This made more people discover his earlier movies, making *Studio Ghibli* and Miyazaki famous worldwide.

As he got older, he wanted to share his life stories and ideas with young people. So, at 82, he released his newest movie, *The Boy and The Heron*. This movie won him his first Golden Globe Award. His hard work and dedication made him a master of animation, inspiring many artists around the world.

UPFLY BOOKS

Photographic acknowledgements (pages 30-31): Amazon.com
All photos of movie posters (pages 30-31) © Studio Ghibli

Other Bilingual Korean-English Books by the Author

Hope you and your little one enjoyed our story! If so, could you spare a moment to rate the book or share your thoughts on Amazon?

Even a quick one-click rating would mean the world to me. It helps me continue creating more educational and fun stories for awesome kids like yours.

Warm regards,
Yeonsil

P.S. Don't forget your free coloring + writing book: upflybooks.com